CHRISTIAN MEDITATION

How to Engage More Deeply in Personal Prayer

Taken from
THE BETTER PART
A Christ-Centered Resource for Personal Prayer

FR. JOHN BARTUNEK, LC, S.Th.D

ministry23

Second Edition
Copyright © 2014 John Bartunek, LC, S.Th.D

Cover image: Mosaics: taken from the Basilica of St. Paul Outside the Walls, Rome

Cover and interior design by Rule29 Creative | www.rule29.com

Gospel text taken from *The Jerusalem Bible* by Alexander Jones, ed., copyright © 1966 by Darton, Longman & Todd, Ltd. and Doubleday, a division of Random House, Inc. Used by permission of Doubleday, a division of Random House, Inc.

Imprimi Potest:
Francisco Mateos, LC

Nihil Obstat
Imprimatur
† Most Reverend Henry J. Mansell
Archbishop of Hartford
June 14, 2007

ISBN: 978-0-9916038-1-7

Printed in the United States of America

10 9 8 7 6 5 4 3 2 1

ministry23

TABLE OF CONTENTS

Foreword

In every era, God provides voices of clarity and light to aid pilgrims in their quest for a deeper relationship with him. The best of them are not necessarily innovators but are innovative in the sense that they bring timeless wisdom within reach of those of their time. Father John Bartunek is one of the best of our time. He is an insightful and faithful guide to those who desire to delve more deeply into the riches of Christ and his Church. A little more about Father John might be in order.

As Father john emerged from his decade of seminary studies, he found himself working within one of the most profound films of our lifetime, The Passion of The Christ. To wrap up his work and provide us with fascinating and multilayered insight into the film, he penned Inside the Passion, the only authorized insider look at this great work of art. Since then, he has blessed tens of thousands of priests, religious and lay-people with his writings and public speaking. His book, *The Better Part – a Christ Centered Resource for Personal Prayer* is Currently in its fourth printing. The book you are reading now is the second derivation from the rich resources found in *The Better Part*. (The first was *Meditations for Mothers*.) Because of the widespread enthusiasm of so many who encounter him, it was clear that we needed to ensure broader access to Father John's insightful and practical overview of authentic Christian meditation – thus this small volume, *A Guide to Christian Meditation: How to Engage More Deeply in Personal Prayer*.

In this book, after a brief historical introduction to Christian meditation, Father John provides both an elegant and memorable method for meditation along with very helpful examples of specifically how to put this method into practice. He manages to do this while keeping our sights on Christ, not the method. His emphasis helps the reader to avoid common and unfortunately popular errors that over-emphasize the means and de-emphasize the all-important end – a deeper relationship with Christ himself.

May your faith, and the faith of those you love, be uniquely blessed by this important work.

Seek Him – Find Him – Follow Him

Dan Burke
Founder of the Avila Institute for Spiritual Formation and Executive Director of EWTN's National Catholic Register

INTRODUCTION

A DIP INTO HISTORY

The method of prayer explained in this book can trace its origins even to the pre-Christian era. The chosen people of the Old Testament appreciated the unique quality of God's Word, and sought to encounter him there. Indeed, Jesus himself spent long nights in prayer, and the words of the Psalmist can be best applied to him: "But his delight is in the law of the Lord, and on his law he meditates day and night" (Ps 1:2). The first generation of Jewish converts brought that tradition with them into the early Christian communities. Pagan converts, many of whom had been educated in the rich literary culture of Hellenism, quickly learned to combine their erudite skills of textual analysis with a resplendent faith in Scripture's inspiration. But the widespread use of the Bible for personal meditation advanced only in fits and starts during the first three Christian centuries, mostly due to the ceaseless waves of violent persecution that repeatedly destabilized Church life.

Nevertheless, personal and small group reading and meditation on Holy Writ was part of the Christian DNA even in those tumultuous centuries. In the year 303, an intrepid Christian woman named Irene was arrested (along with her two sisters) for refusing to worship idols. While in prison, a search of her house uncovered some forbidden copies of New Testament writings (at that time, forbidding the possession of Scripture was a tactic aimed at suffocating the growing Christian Church). Brought before the governor for interrogation and asked who had ordered her to keep the documents in direct defiance of the emperor's edict, Irene gave brave testimony: "Almighty

God, who has commanded us to love him unto death. For that reason we prefer to be burnt alive rather than give up the Holy Scriptures and betray him…. They were hidden in the house, but we dared not produce them: we were in great trouble because we could no longer read them day and night as we had been accustomed to do."[1]

Once the Age of Persecution had passed, this love for the inspired Word became the heart of the monastic movement in the Christian East and West. Creating a stable, austere community life based on work, prayer, and practicing the Christian virtues, monasticism fostered an environment in which copies of the Bible could be made more easily and the texts studied and meditated over more readily and frequently by a greater number of people (monasteries and convents often had hundreds of members from all strata of society). Thus the practice of *lectio divina* (divine reading) developed.

In these centuries, the majority of church-going Christians had only rudimentary (if any) reading skills, and there would sometimes be only one Bible for an entire parish community. This would be kept in a common room, chained to a table, rather like telephone books in twentieth century phone booths. Even so, the Word of God was amply communicated in both sermons and works of art, and Christians with just a smattering of formal education could, therefore, often boast of a thorough familiarity with the Scriptures.

---

[1] *See Alban Butler,* Lives of the Saints, *original edition (first printing, 1798-1800, London and Newcastle), entry for April 4.*

Only with the advent of the printing press, however, towards the middle of the second Christian millennium, did it become possible for average Christians to own personal copies of the Bible. At the same time, the turbulence of early modern European life created a social environment in which *lectio divina* as practiced by the monks was less easily emulated. Multiple new methods (and variations on old methods) of meditating on the Bible emerged, and the surest ones stood the test of time. The common elements of those form the substance of what is presented here, and they are explained in light of the peculiar challenges to prayer posed by a mass-media-saturated social milieu.[2]

THE IMPORTANCE OF PERSONAL PRAYER

Conscientious Christians pray. Their typical days, weeks, months, and years are seasoned with prayer – traditional prayers, liturgical prayers, spontaneous prayers. They make prayer commitments, giving structure and consistency to their faith journey. Prayer keeps Christians united to the Vine, so their lives can bear the fruit both they and Christ long for.[3]

Among the most basic prayer commitments is one that can have more bearing on your life than any other, because it is more personalized: the daily meditation. Certainly you can't

---

[2] *For a more specific summary of contributors to the history of mental prayer, see Adolphe Tanquerey,* The Spiritual Life, *no. 665. For a more thorough treatment, see Louis Bouyer,* History of Christian Spirituality.

[3] *"I am the vine, and you are the branches. He who dwells in me, as I dwell in him, bears much fruit; for apart from me you can do nothing" (Jn 15:5).*

mature as a Christian without the sacramental life, just as crops can't mature without sunlight and soil. And the various devotional and vocal prayers that punctuate your day keep you strong and focused amid the unrelenting blows of the unchristian culture all around you. But, as generations of saints and sinners have found out, that is not enough.

Without the daily renewal and deepening of your personal relationship with Jesus Christ that happens especially through meditation, sooner or later routine sets in. You get into a rut. Your prayers get mechanical, your sacramental life slides into hollow ritualism, and before you know it, your faith gets side-lined and you get dragged back into the rat race in some form or other. Daily meditation keeps your faith, that pearl of great price,[4] lively, supple, and relevant. It irrigates the soil of your soul, making your sacramental life more fruitful, keeping your other prayer commitments meaningful, and continually open-ing up new vistas along the path to spiritual maturity. This is why spiritual writers through the ages have so consistently emphasized the importance of meditation, also known as mental prayer, since it is a deeply interior way of praying. Here is what two doctors of the Church have to say about it:

> He who neglects mental prayer needs not a devil to carry him to hell, but he brings himself there with his own hands (*St. Theresa of Avila*).

> It is morally impossible for him who neglects meditation to live without sin (*St. Alphonsus Ligouri*).

---

[4] *"Again, the kingdom of heaven is like a merchant looking for fine pearls; when he finds one of great value he goes and sells everything he owns and buys it"* (Mt 13.45-46).

> And by experience we see that many persons who recite a great
> number of vocal prayers, the Office and the Rosary, fall into sin,
> and continue to live in sin. But he who attends to mental prayer
> scarcely ever falls into sin, and should he have the misfortune of
> falling into it, he will hardly continue to live in so miserable a state;
> he will either give up mental prayer, or renounce sin. Meditation
> and sin cannot stand together. However abandoned a soul may be,
> if she perseveres in meditation, God will bring her to salvation (*St.
> Alphonsus Ligouri*).

The daily meditation, in other words, is not an optional extra
for super-Christians; it's every Christian's bread and but-
ter. Without it, your Christian identity shrivels. But it's not
enough just to do a daily meditation; you need to learn to do
it better and better. Maturity in the spiritual life depends to
a great extent on constantly going deeper in your personal
prayer life. The law of life is growth, so if your capacity for
mental prayer isn't growing, your life with Christ is in danger
of wasting away.[5]

THE BENEFITS OF CHRISTIAN MEDITATION

Used well, *A Guide to Christian Meditation* will help you
discover at least three things:

1. HOW YOU PRAY BEST. Prayer is similar to walking. To
walk, everyone has to follow the same principles of physics
– friction, gravity, muscle propulsion, momentum. And yet,

---

[5]*This intensely personal prayer – the Christian meditation – contributes significantly to the communal
life of the Church. As our personal friendship with Christ develops, we become more mature and fruitful
members of his Body, the Church. Therefore, although this book focuses on the personal encounter with
Christ in meditation, it does not mean to belittle the ecclesial nature of the Christian vocation. The two
aspects are complementary and intertwined.*

even though the principles are the same, everyone's walk is a little bit different. When babies learn to walk, they start out clumsy and awkward, until they develop the rhythm and style proper to their body type, personality, and environment. Meditation follows a similar pattern: the same principles for all, activated uniquely by each. *A Guide to Christian Meditation* can help you wherever you happen to be on the spectrum.

2. **THE DIMENSIONS OF CHRIST:** (his characteristics, actions, words, sufferings) that speak most profoundly to your soul. The heart of Christianity is each believer's friendship with Jesus Christ, and friendship is never generic. If you read the lives of the saints, you quickly discover how each one's holiness has its own, unique flavor – St. Francis' friendship with Christ was different than St. Dominic's, because St. Francis and St. Dominic were different. Every person has a unique personality, so each person will relate to Christ uniquely. God created you to know him as only you can know him. Christian meditation is designed to help you uncover and develop the distinctiveness of your friendship with Christ, without which you will always feel more restless and dissatisfied than necessary.

3. **THE INESTIMABLE VALUE OF A DEEP PRAYER LIFE.** Every Christian has a responsibility to become an expert in prayer. Without a mature prayer life, you cannot become a mature Christian, in which case you will never

discover the authentic Christian joy, wisdom, and fruitfulness that flow from being fully formed in Christ.[6] This expertise in prayer comes only from the Holy Spirit, who uses two training methods:

First, he instructs you in prayer through the experience of others. Through the ages, the Church and its saints have produced a whole library of accessible, practical, and inspiring books on prayer. You'll want to read them and study them. All Christians who take their friendship with Christ seriously should regularly read good books (and plenty of good articles) on prayer or the spiritual life.[7] *A Guide to Christian Meditation* will serve as a refresher course on the central principles of Christian meditation, something you can refer to in order to keep your meditation in shape.

Second, the Holy Spirit makes you an expert in prayer when you actually pray. You need to dive into the pool and splash around so that your coach can teach you to swim. And so, if you are just starting out in Christian meditation, this little guide can help you lay a firm foundation.

Many Christians – even committed, well-formed Christians – reach a plateau in their prayer life because their meditation stays at the level of reflective spiritual reading, even when

---

[6]*"My dear children, for whom I am again in the pains of childbirth until Christ is formed in you…"* (Galatians 4:19); *"…to build up the Body of Christ, until we all reach unity in faith and knowledge of the Son of God and form the perfect man, fully mature with the fullness of Christ himself. If we live by the truth and in love, we shall grow completely into Christ"* (Eph 4: 12-13, 15).
[7] *See the Appendix for a list of excellent books on prayer and the spiritual life.*

their soul is ready to go higher (this distinction is explained more fully later).

A Guide to Christian Meditation is a tool for knowing, loving, and following Christ more wholeheartedly, which is what God is hoping for, your soul is thirsting for, and all prayer is striving for. It will review in detail the fundamental principles, steps, and difficulties of Christian meditation, and it will equip you to do a check-up on your own prayer life.

Be forewarned – Christ never promised that following him would be easy. In fact, he promised it wouldn't. The spiritual life is full of mystery. You find yourself on unfamiliar ground when you trust God to lead you to richer pastures. Often it is much more comfortable to keep doing what you already know how to do, like Martha, who busied herself in the kitchen when Jesus and the apostles dropped by for dinner. Her sister Mary put normal activities on hold for a little while instead and sat at Jesus' feet, drinking in his wisdom, his love, and his beauty. When Martha complained that Mary was being lazy and impractical, Jesus smiled at her and said:

> "Martha, Martha. You worry and fret about so many things, and yet few are needed, indeed only one. It is Mary who has chosen the better part, and it is not to be taken from her" (*Lk 10:41-42*).

The Fundamentals of
Christian Meditation

GOD'S IDEA OF PRAYER

What do you picture yourself doing when you start to pray? What image, conscious or not, do you have in mind? Maybe you see yourself merely fulfilling a duty, as when you mechanically recited the Pledge of Allegiance at the start of homeroom in elementary school. Maybe you see prayer as an exercise in self-mastery and self-help, an activity – like yoga, aerobics, or weightlifting – that keeps you fit. Whatever you *think* you are doing when you pray affects the *way* in which you do it. So the more your idea of prayer matches God's, the better.

Prayer at its most basic level is conversation with God. This seems obvious, but it harbors an awesome reality. To converse with someone implies that that someone wants to pay attention to you, otherwise you have a monologue, not a conversation. The mere existence of prayer, then, implies that God is paying attention, that he is interested in spending time with you. Christian prayer is an invitation from God to the one who prays – it starts with God, not with you.

The whole Christian edifice is built on this simple but awe-inspiring reality. The Catechism highlights it in its very first numbers: "At every time and in every place, God draws close to man… God never ceases to draw man to himself" (1, 27). God is always drawing close to you, and he is always drawing you closer to him. That means he is always thinking of you, just like the Good Shepherd who is always thinking of and watching over his sheep. Prayer starts here.

You are the lost and hungry sheep; God is the shepherd who knows what you desire and need and is guiding you to the lush fields and cool, refreshing waters of his Truth and Love. The shepherd sees the big picture, the whole landscape, the weather, the seasons, the dangers and the opportunities; the sheep can only focus on this little patch of grass here and then that one over there. Prayer is the Good Shepherd, wise and loving, guiding the hungry, shortsighted, and needy sheep.

God is the real protagonist of Christian prayer. Prayer is the soul's response to God's initiative. The essence of Christian prayer is relationship. As the Catechism puts it:

> "Great is the mystery of the faith!"… This mystery, then, requires that the faithful believe in it, that they celebrate it, and that they live from it in a vital and personal relationship with the living and true God. *This relationship is prayer* (2558, emphasis added).

Prayer, then, is more than just a dry religious duty, more than self-centered and self-sufficient self-help techniques; Christian prayer is a friendship with God in Christ. It's being led by the Good Shepherd to ever richer pastures in the Father's kingdom.[1]

CHRISTIAN PRAYER: EMINENTLY CHRIST-CENTERED

What matters most in prayer, then, is docility to that Good Shepherd, listening honestly, and responding honestly. God is already at work; you have only to hear and heed his voice.

---

[1] *This definition of prayer – as an ongoing relationship – doesn't eliminate the need for particular times dedicated to conversing exclusively with God. There's no better way to make a relationship grow cold than by not spending quality time together. As the Catechism puts it, "… we cannot pray 'at all times' if we do not pray at specific times, consciously willing it" (2697).*

So how does he speak to you?

> At various times in the past and in various different ways, God
> spoke to our ancestors through the prophets; but in our own time,
> the last days, he has spoken to us through his Son, the Son that he
> has appointed to inherit everything and through whom he made
> everything there is. He is the radiant light of God's glory and the
> perfect copy of his nature, sustaining the universe by his power-
> ful command… That is why all you who are holy brothers and
> have had the same heavenly call should *turn your minds to Jesus,*
> the apostle and the high priest of our religion (Heb 1:1-3, 3:1,
> emphasis added).

Christian prayer consists of that "turning your minds to Jesus,"
the Jesus who comes to us through the revelation of the Gospels,
the good news of the "boundless riches" (Eph 3:8) of Christ.

The riches of Christ are boundless because Christ is God-
revealing-himself-to-man and God is infinite. If you want to
get to know someone, it is not enough to learn *about* him
from the outside; he has to open his mind and heart to you
so that you can really get to know *him,* his thoughts and
desires, his yearnings, his way of seeing things, his concerns.
Interpersonal knowledge, the knowledge of friendship, can
only come through personal revelation. Christ is God-reveal-
ing-himself-to-you, offering you his friendship.

Only Christianity is so bold as to claim that in Christ we can
become God's friends, because only Christianity offers a God
who becomes man, a Good Shepherd who becomes a lamb
in order to win the hearts of his sheep:

> I shall not call you servants any more, because a servant does

not know his master's business; I call you friends, because I have made known to you everything I have learnt from my Father (Jn 15:15).

True Christian prayer, therefore, is Christ-centered prayer. Above all, it consists in contemplating and conversing with Christ, the "one Mediator" between man and God (1 Tm 2:5). In prayer you sit at the feet of the Master, listening, learning, and loving. Prayer comes before action; the active life, for a Christian, overflows from the contemplative life. Christ taught this clearly when he gently reprimanded the busy and active Martha for resenting her sister Mary's preference for *the better part*.[2]

CHRISTIAN PRAYER: INTENSELY PERSONAL But Christian prayer is also intensely personal. This friendship that God has struck up with you is unique, because you are unique. Christ is not an abstract concept; he is a real person. Your friendship with him will be different than mine, because your life experience, your personality, your problems and talents and worries and dreams are different from mine, and all those things go into a friendship.

In prayer, the Good Shepherd calls his sheep individually: "… one by one he calls his own sheep and leads them out. When he has brought out his flock, he goes ahead of them, and the sheep follow because they know his voice" (Jn 10:3-4).

Prayer is Christ speaking to you in your heart, revealing

---

[2] *"Martha, Martha, you worry and fret about so many things, and yet few are needed, indeed only one. It is Mary who has chosen **the better part**; it is not to be taken from her"* (Lk 10:42, emphasis added).

himself to you in accordance with what he knows you need to discover, to know, to see. At the same time, prayer is your attentive listening to that revelation, your response to what he reveals, and the trusting, reciprocal revelation of your heart – your needs, your hopes, your desires – to him.

In this mysterious, beautiful exchange, the Holy Spirit is the bridge between Christ's heart and yours: "Now instead of the spirit of the world, we have received the Spirit that comes from God, to teach us to understand the gifts that he has given us" (1 Cor 2:12). The Holy Spirit guides you from within, into the arms of Christ, the Good Shepherd of your soul.

If you want to continue to discover and follow God's path for your life, this intensely personal prayer is a necessary element in your spiritual life. While you are here on earth, God always has more he wants to reveal to you and teach you; he has more he wants to do in your soul, making it the masterpiece that he envisioned from the moment of your creation. He also has more work he wants you to do, work that will bear eternal fruit to his glory and to your temporal and everlasting happiness. All of this, however, requires that you grow closer to him, and without a deep, personal prayer life, you simply can't.

TYPES OF PRAYER

The Catechism points out three basic types of personal (as distinct from liturgical) prayer: vocal, meditative, and contemplative, all of which have a place in the life of every Christian.

VOCAL PRAYER Vocal prayer consists in reciting ready-made prayers, either silently or aloud, uniting the intention of your heart to the meaning of the words. This is the kind of prayer recited together before a meal or the prayers often used each morning to offer the day to God. The words of these prayers help you express your faith and that conscious expression in turn reinforces and exercises your faith. All Christians should have their favorite vocal prayers, the ones that resonate best with their own experience of Christ, the ones they can go back to in moments of dryness, sickness, or difficulty.

MEDITATIVE PRAYER Meditative prayer is less formulaic. It consists in lifting the heart and mind to God through focused reflection on some truth of God's revelation. It involves the intellect, the imagination, the memory, the emotions – the whole person.

In meditation, as you turn your gaze to God's self-revelation in Christ, you are moved to respond to what you discover there, and you converse with God in the silence of your own heart, using words that flow naturally from your reflection.

Reflecting on the beauty of God's creation, for example, may move your heart to expressions of gratitude, wonder, and praise. Reflecting on the sufferings of Christ during his crucifixion may move your heart to expressions of humility, repentance, or sorrow. The essence of Christian meditation is this exchange between God and the soul; this intimate conversation can take an infinite variety of forms.

Whatever form it takes, however, meditation puts the soul in contact with the eternal truths, with the love and goodness of God in its myriad manifestations, and thus it *nourishes* the soul. Just as the body needs food and water, the soul feeds on truth and love. This reality is categorically ignored by today's secularized, materialistic culture which denies the existence of moral and spiritual truth and reduces love to mere feelings. Meditative prayer, however, only makes sense in light of this reality. Your soul, your intellect, and your will yearn for the true and the good as much as your body yearns for solid food and fresh drink. "Happy those who hunger and thirst for what is right: they shall be satisfied" (Mt 5:6).

Meditation's loving dialogue between God and you praying in Christ opens your soul to experience the highest, most nourishing truth of all: the total, transforming, unconditional love with which God himself regards you. This experience literally feeds the soul, enlivening its own capacity for love, energizing it, and inspiring it.

Meditative prayer, then, exercises the great Christian virtues of faith, hope, and love, helping the soul that has been wounded by sin, both original and personal, to rehabilitate its capacity to discover, experience, and communicate God's own truth, goodness, and beauty.

Christian meditation differs essentially from transcendental meditation and other New Age centering techniques.[3] Chris-

---

[3]Some Christian spiritualities have tried to adopt so-called centering prayer techniques from non-Christian sources. Although some of these techniques can be incorporated into the first stage of the meditation

tian meditation is Christ-centered, a loving dialogue between Christ and the soul that deepens your friendship with Christ. It starts with the Holy Spirit urging you to pursue a greater knowledge and love of Christ and ends with your renewed commitment to follow and imitate Christ in the unique circumstances of your daily life.

Transcendental meditation, on the other hand, is self-centered. Instead of a dialogue with God, an opening of the soul to God, it consists primarily in calming the many passions of the soul, creating a self-induced interior tranquility and focus that overflows in certain types of feelings. The goal of transcendental meditation is to withdraw from the complexities of life in order to experience emotional tranquility; the goal of Christian meditation is to know, love, and follow Jesus Christ more completely, to discover and embrace God's will for you more and more each day.

CONTEMPLATIVE PRAYER Contemplative prayer consists of a more passive (and more sublime) experience of God. If meditation is the soul's inspired quest to discover God, contemplation is God's lifting of the soul into himself, so that it effortlessly basks in the divine light. It is the soul's silent gazing upon the grandeur of God.

(Concentrate), they are unnecessary and can often be harmful. They frequently result in becoming ends in themselves; the one praying uses them to create certain higher emotional states as if those states were the goal of prayer. Christian prayer is interpersonal; centering prayer is really no more than a technique for calming oneself. It originated in the context of eastern transcendental asceticism, and these techniques are ill-suited for Christian prayer. For a more complete discussion of this issue, see the Pontifical Council for Interreligious Dialogue's document from 3 February 2003, "Jesus Christ: The Bearer of the Water of Life," available on the Vatican Web site, www.vatican.va.

Often meditation leads to contemplation – the line of demarcation is hazy. When you find yourself lifted into silent contemplation during your meditation, there is no need to fear. The practice of Christian meditation gradually purifies the heart and familiarizes it with the voice and the ways of God so that, little by little, the soul is made more docile to the promptings of God and God can reveal himself more and more completely.

All three types of prayer – vocal, meditative, and contemplative – put the Christian in contact with the grassy pastures and refreshing waters of God's grace. They are the sure paths along which the Good Shepherd faithfully leads his sheep.

MEDITATION VS. SPIRITUAL READING

Sometimes following ready-made meditations[4] is an excellent way to pray. The structure helps you stay focused, the content is sure to be healthy, and the easy access motivates you to keep up a regular prayer life. But ready-made meditations also have a disadvantage. They can become nothing more than spiritual reading.

Spiritual reading refers to reading texts – books, articles, homilies, essays – that teach you about the spiritual life; it's like taking a class from whoever wrote the book. It enlightens your conscience by helping you see yourself and the world around you from a Christian perspective. As such, it is an essential ingredient for growth as a Christian. Just as

---

[4]*Like those published daily through the Regnum Christi Web site, www.regnumchristi.org*

historians are always reading about history and teachers are always informing themselves about developments in pedagogy, so Christians should constantly be refining and expanding their understanding of how to be a follower of Christ.[5]

Christian meditation also involves an effort to better understand Christ and the Christian life, so it often yields results similar to those of spiritual reading, especially for beginners in the spiritual life. Primarily, though, meditation is a matter of the heart more than the intellect; it's like taking a leisurely walk with Christ, your friend.

The focused reflection at the core of meditation opens the soul to hear, not an abstract truth about the Christian life, but a particular word that God, the Good Shepherd, wishes to speak to you in the unique *here and now* of your life. When you tune into this word, this truth, this message from the Holy Spirit, your heart is drawn to stay with it, to consider it, to savor it. Savoring it in turn stirs your heart to express itself and give voice to your most intimate, personal yearnings, hopes, affections, or needs. In this conversation, you are actually *exercising* the Christian virtues of faith, hope, and love; you are exercising your friendship. In spiritual reading, you are learning, you are gaining knowledge. Both spiritual reading and meditation are useful – indeed, both are necessary for a healthy spiritual life – but it's important not to confuse them.

---

[5]*Regnum Christi members' daily Gospel Reflection falls into this category of spiritual reading. It keeps you constantly in touch with Christ's criteria and example so that throughout the day you can keep aligning your thoughts, attitudes, and actions with Christ's. It's like rebooting your computer – it clears away the interior clutter that accumulates during the day.*

Although ready-made meditations have many advantages, they also have the disadvantage of easily morphing into spiritual reading. You lead a busy life with little time to prepare your daily meditation. You have committed to doing it though, so you faithfully gather the daily meditation from the Web site and read it over between errands or before speeding off to work. It keeps you in touch with spiritual things and gives you new insights or renews old ones, but because it's a complete, self-contained meditation, you easily slip into the spiritual reading mode. Instead of using the points of reflection as springboards for focused personal reflection, attentive listening to the Holy Spirit, and intimate, heart-to-heart conversation with Christ, you simply read, understand, agree, and move on.

Spiritual reading is valuable; it will help you grow closer to Christ. The Lord is happy that you make time for him. And yet unless you learn to go deeper, to personalize your prayer more, you will limit your growth in virtue. God wants to make you into the saint he created you to be, but that requires a more personal, heart-to-heart prayer life. He wants to give you that grace, but he needs you to give him the chance.

THE 4-STEP STRUCTURE OF YOUR MEDITATION

AN OVERVIEW Perhaps you are already familiar with the general meditation structure recommended in *The Better Part,* from which this guide is taken. Drawn from the long-lasting and fruitful traditions of Ignatian and Carmelite spirituality, it follows four steps: *Concentrate, Consider, Converse, and Commit*.

Sometimes a meditation flows easily, following these steps one after another without a hitch. Other times tiredness, distractions, or temptations plague you so persistently that each step demands a heroic effort. Still other times, the steps blend together and your conversation with God happens almost spontaneously. This shows that the four-step method of meditation is not an end in itself, nor is it an arbitrary concoction. Rather, this method sets out the basic elements of any heart-to-heart conversation with God, as gleaned from experience and theology. In so doing, it provides a dependable framework for your personal encounter with God in spite of the persistent and sometimes almost overwhelming obstacles to prayer that surface.

At first you may find it awkward to follow the steps. You may feel tempted to fall back into the less demanding pattern of spiritual reading, but as your prayer life deepens, this simple structure becomes second nature. When kids first learn to play basketball, they have to master the basic skills – dribbling, shooting, passing – one at a time. As they improve, they develop the ability to combine these fundamentals into a smooth, seamless whole. Eventually, they are free to really play. Assimilating the structure of your meditation happens a lot like that.

MAKING PROGRESS Keep in mind that growth in the spiritual life and in prayer takes time and consistent effort. Sometimes you may feel that you are making great progress;

then suddenly you seem to have a relapse. Other times you may feel that you are making no progress at all, and then unexpectedly spring forward.

This isn't because God whimsically comes and goes. Rather, he is mysteriously guiding you through a gradual purification of the selfish tendencies deeply embedded in your soul. Points of view, emotional patterns, mental landscapes – all of these, because of original and personal sin, are shot through with myriad forms of self-centeredness that clog the flow of God's grace. Thus, learning to pray better is like turning a wild, overgrown plot of rocky ground into an ordered, fragrant, beautiful garden – God supplies the sunshine, the water, and the soil, but you still have to dig and plant and prune, and then keep on digging and planting and pruning…. Think of the four steps of the meditation as your gardening tools.

Understanding the reasons behind each step will help you follow them more peacefully and fruitfully. These steps can also be useful reference points as you discuss your prayer life during spiritual direction. A clear idea of these elements will make your ongoing reading about prayer more fruitful as well. Remember, every Christian should steadily strive to become an expert in prayer, since prayer is that "vital and personal relationship with the living and true God"[6] – the relationship which gives life itself and all of life's components their deepest, most authentic, and most satisfying meaning. Below is an explanation of each

---

[6] *Catechism of the Catholic Church*, 2558

step. After the explanation you will find the full text of a real, sample meditation with all the steps identified.

STEP 1: CONCENTRATE

This involves drawing your attention away from the exterior activities and practical concerns that tend to monopolize your thoughts and turning your attention to God, who is already paying full attention to you. You refresh your awareness of God's presence which tends to be drowned out by the din of the daily grind.

Useful in this step are the traditional preparatory acts of faith, hope, and love, wherein you lift your heart and mind to God, tuning your attention to God's wavelength. You can use ready-made texts for your preparatory acts, compose your own, voice them spontaneously, or combine all three methods. This guide provides some sample preparatory acts. The morning prayers from your prayer book can make for good preparatory acts as well.

The most important part of this step is not the actual words you use. Rather, you need to remind yourself of the truths that underlie your relationship with God, reviving your most basic Christian attitudes. The goal of this step is fourfold:

- *Recall that God is truly present*, listening to you, paying attention. Remember that God is all-powerful, all-wise, all-loving, and that he knows you intimately and cares for you more than you care for yourself. He deserves your praise, your attention, and your time.

- *Recall that God has something he wants to say to you.* He has a word for you today. He knows what you are struggling with in the short term and the long; he knows what the day will have in store for you; he knows the path he has marked out for your growth in happiness and holiness. He is going to work in your soul while you pray, whether you feel anything or not. Remember, your daily meditation isn't just your idea, it is a prayer commitment linked with your particular vocation in the Church, and your vocation comes from God. You know without a doubt that God has something to say to you during this time because he made the appointment.

- *Recall that you need to hear that word.* You are dependent on God for everything, starting with your existence. You have failed and sinned many times; the duties and mission you have in life are beyond your own natural capabilities; you are surrounded by morally and spiritually corrupting influences, by a variety of temptations… In short, you are a dependent, created being damaged by sin: you need God's grace.

- *Renew your desire to hear that word.* You want to follow him. You believe that he is the Lord, your Savior, your Friend, and your Guide. You have committed your life to him; you have put your trust in him.

In this context, part of your concentration will consist in asking God for the grace you feel you most need, in accordance with your program of spiritual work. Sometimes this is called the petition or the fruit of the meditation. Asking God for this grace brings all those basic attitudes into play. At the same time, however, you leave the reins in his hands, knowing that he will guide you in hidden ways to the rich pastures he has in store for you.

Whether you use your favorite traditional acts of faith, hope, and love to achieve this concentration matters less than simply achieving it. Sometimes it is enough to call to mind your favorite verse or Psalm from the Bible to activate all these sentiments; sometimes it's enough to remember the beauties of nature or one of your most powerful experiences of God.

As the weeks and months pass by, you may need to vary the way you concentrate in order to avoid falling into a dry routine where you say all the right words, but in fact fail to turn your heart and mind to God. Without that, without concentrating on God, it will be nearly impossible for you to really enter into conversation with him and hear what he wants to tell you – your prayer will turn into a self-centered monologue or an empty, wordy shell.

At times these preparatory acts may launch you directly into a heart-to-heart conversation with the Lord, bypassing Step 2, *Consider*. When this happens, don't feel obliged to backtrack; the material of your preparatory acts has provided the Holy Spirit with all he needed to lift you right into Step 3, *Converse*.

Concentrating on God doesn't mean ignoring the realities of your life. Your worries and concerns and yearnings and dreams and challenges should all enter into your meditation. But they come into play within the context of your heart-to-heart conversation with the God who loves you. This is the difference between simply worrying and actually praying about something. When you sit down to have a cup of coffee with a close friend, your worries and dreams don't disappear, but they fall into line behind the attention you give to your friend and the attention your friend gives to you.

Related to Step 1 is your choice of time and place for your daily meditation. These factors affect your ability to *Concentrate*.

- *The time.* Most spiritual writers agree that doing your meditation in the morning helps imbue your coming day's activities with their true Christian meaning. Your mind is fresh, so it's easier to focus. And a morning meditation can give unity and direction to your daily duties by reminding you of your life's mission (to know, love, and follow Christ) and preparing you to meet the day's un-expected (or expected) challenges. With a little effort and creativity, you can usually make room for the morning meditation, whether it's ten, fifteen, twenty minutes, or even half an hour. (If you have any doubts about the proper length of your daily meditation, you should discuss them with a confes-sor or spiritual director.) If the morning is simply impossible, try to find some space in your day when you know you won't be interrupted – a time when you will be able to give your best to your prayer. Use the same time slot each day as much as possible. Try not to just squeeze it in; give your best time to God.

- *The place.* Where you do your meditation should be out of range of interruptions and conducive to your conversation with God. Some people prefer their church or a chapel with the Blessed Sacrament; others prefer a particular room at home. Here again creativity and practical convenience come into play. A businessman in Boston stops at a cemetery on his way to work and does his meditation walking among the tombs and monuments (during the summer) – it's the only place where he can consistently dodge interruptions. Avoid changing places frequently in a vain search for the perfect atmosphere; the place doesn't make the prayer, it is only a means to help.

- *On special days or during certain periods* (e.g., vacation, Holy Week), you may find it helpful to change your normal place and time of prayer. Temporary, planned changes can keep you from falling into a dull routine.

If you habitually find it hard to concentrate at the start of your meditation, check on the status of your *remote* and *proximate* preparation. These terms refer to what you do outside of your meditation that affects what happens during your meditation.

- *Remote preparation.* You don't meditate in a vacuum. The more you live in God's presence during the rest of day, seeking his will and finding other times here and there to pray (vocal prayers, the Rosary, examination of conscience), the easier it will be for you to turn your heart and soul to God at the start of the meditation. This is your remote preparation.

- *Proximate preparation.* You will also avoid a plethora of distractions if you get your meditation materials (the book you will be using, your notebook or journal for writing down thoughts) ready the night before. You can even briefly look over the passage you will be meditating on before you go to bed; this too primes the prayer-pump. This is your proximate preparation.

Jesus himself explained the step of concentrating simply and vividly: "When you pray, go to your private room and, when you have shut your door, pray to your Father who is in that secret place, and your Father who sees all that is done in secret will reward you" (Mt 6:6). The prophet Elijah discovered this truth when the Lord spoke to him on the mountain:

Then the Lord himself went by. There came a mighty wind, so strong it tore the mountains and shattered the rocks before the

Lord. But the Lord was not in the wind. After the wind came an earthquake. But the Lord was not in the earthquake. After the earthquake came a fire. But the Lord was not in the fire. And after the fire there came the sound of a gentle breeze (1 Kgs 19:11-12).

Concentrate, the first step of your meditation, involves shutting the door on the storms and tumult of daily life for a time, so that you can hear the Lord's still, small voice that whispers in your heart like a gentle breeze.

STEP 2: CONSIDER

With life's hustle and bustle in its proper place, you are ready to listen to God's message for you today. Here you take time for focused reflection on God's words, usually as they are found in Scripture – although you can also turn to other spiritual writings, the works of the saints, Church documents, and even sacred art as texts for consideration. Gradually, with the help of your confessor or spiritual director, you will find the kind of material that helps you most, in accordance with your program of spiritual work.

During this stage, you slowly and thoughtfully read the text you will be meditating on. You reflect on it, you examine it, you dig into it. You read it again, searching to discover what God is saying to you through it in the *here and now* of your life. You exercise your whole mind: intellect, imagination, and memory. You involve your emotions, relating the passage to your own life experience.

This type of meditative consideration differs from study. The goal of meditation is not necessarily to learn new truths, but to give God a chance to make the truths you need most sink deeper into your mind and heart. Considering a truth involves understanding it more clearly, more deeply. But it also involves savoring it, gazing upon it, basking in it.

This step poses a challenge for victims of the media age. The human mind is capable of wonder, contemplation, and reflection, but when the principle source of information is mass media, these capacities can atrophy. Mass media stimulates the surface of the mind, but the constant, rapid flow of images and information militates against going deep. Meditation provides a respite from frenzied mental stimulation and gives the soul a chance to simply love and be loved in the intimacy of a spiritual embrace.

Just as it takes the body time to digest food and benefit from its nutrients, so the soul needs time to take in and assimilate the healing, enlightening, and strengthening truths God has revealed through Christ's Gospel. Just as it takes long hours in the sun for plants to photosynthesize so they can grow and flourish, so the soul needs extended exposure to the light of Christ in order for God's grace to purify, enliven, and heal it.

God knows which truths you need to dwell on; part of the *Consider* stage is searching for them. God speaks most often in whispers, not storms, and so you have to move forward in your meditation calmly, gently, hunting for the insight God wishes to give you. This is one of the most mysterious aspects of meditation. Christ the Good Shepherd guides you towards the rich pastures and refreshing waters of his truth and grace, sometimes along an easy path and other times along a steep and difficult path. For each day when it is easy to find and savor God's word for you, there is another day when your meditation seems to entail nothing but work.

This exercise of seeking out where God is speaking to your soul turns Christian meditation into a quest: "Meditation is a prayerful quest engaging thought, imagination, emotion, and desire."[7] Usually, as you read and reflect on the subject of your meditation, you can detect where the Holy Spirit wants you to stop and consider simply by the reaction of your heart.

In a garden full of beautiful flowers and plants, you stay longer in front of one because you find that its beauty resonates more deeply with you. In a gallery of magnificent works of art, you are drawn to one or two of them more powerfully, because they have something to say to you, in the here and now of your life, that the others don't.

Likewise with meditation. If you have done your best to focus the powers of your soul on God in the *Concentrate* step, as you begin to *Consider* the material for your meditation, one or two things will catch your attention; they will jump out at you, as if they were highlighted. It may be a phrase in the actual text or an idea that comes to your mind. That highlight is the guiding hand of the Good Shepherd. Thus the Holy Spirit gently leads you to the spiritual food your soul needs most.

---

[7] *Catechism of the Catholic Church,* 2723

If nothing strikes you right away, you can intensify your consideration by asking questions.

- For instance, if you are considering a passage from the Gospel, you can enter into the scene by asking basic, journalistic questions: *Who is here? What are they feeling, doing and saying? When is this event taking place? Where is it happening and what does everything look like? Why is it happening in this way? How is each person reacting?* As you enter more deeply into the living Word of God, the Holy Spirit will guide your mind and heart to the point he wants you to consider. When you find it, savor it.

- Another approach uses less imagination and more reason. You can begin to consider the material of your meditation by asking analytical questions: *What strikes me about this passage? What does this mean? What does it tell me about Christ, the Church, the meaning of life?* And after having looked at it in the abstract, make it personal – *What does it mean for me? What is Christ saying to me in the here and now of my life? How is this truth relevant to my own struggles, my own mission and vocation, my own program of spiritual work, my own friendship with Christ, and my own journey of faith?*

It may take almost the whole time you have set aside for meditation to discover the point God wants you to consider. This is not a cause for discouragement or frustration: during the search, the quest, you are exercising all of the Christian virtues – faith in God, hope in his goodness, love for him, humility, and trust. The more difficult the search, the more these virtues are being exercised; the Holy Spirit is giving you a vigorous spiritual workout. God knows just what you need and how to guide you; he is the Good Shepherd.

Sometimes you never seem to find the highlights at all. In these cases too, God is at work. Never doubt his active presence. When the material you have set aside for consideration doesn't yield any insights worth savoring, you can feel free to turn to your favorite biblical images, your favorite vocal prayers, or your favorite verses – go back to the waters and pastures that have nourished you in the past. All mature Christians gradually discover certain truths of the Gospel that can always provide food for their souls.

At times you may find so many highlights that you feel overwhelmed. Stay calm. Don't rush. Take one flower, one painting, one highlight at a time and exhaust it, delight in it until your heart is saturated. Only then move on to the next highlight. As long as your consideration continues to move your heart, stay with that point, like a bee extracting nectar from a blossom. Never move on just because you feel like you're supposed to. Prayer is a personal conversation, not a generic connect-the-dots operation.

STEP 3: CONVERSE

Precisely because Christian prayer is interpersonal, your consideration of the truths of Christ, your basking in his light, is never only passive. In an embrace, both people receive and both people give. In the embrace of prayer, you receive the truth and grace of God's revelation and you give your personal response. As soon as the truth you are considering touches your heart, it will stir a response. This is the heart of your meditation.

If you are considering the wonders of God's creation, you may be moved to respond with words or sentiments of praise: *How great you are, my God! How beautiful you must be if your creation is this awe-inspiring….*

If you are considering God's mercy, you may be moved to respond with contrition, remorse, and sorrow for your sins: *You are so good and generous, so patient; why, Lord, am I so slow to trust you, why am I so selfish? Forgive me, Lord, a thousand times, please forgive me; I know you have, you do, and you will, but still I ask you to forgive me, I am sorry….*

If you are considering some of the many gifts he has given you, like your faith, your family, or the Eucharist, you may be moved to express gratitude: *Thank you, Father, from the bottom of my heart, I really mean it, thank you. Thank you for giving me life, and for showing me the meaning of life, and for saving me from so many dangers, so many sins….*

Whatever you may be considering, sooner or later, like a child in the presence of his benevolent and powerful father, you will probably find yourself asking for good things from

God: *O my Lord, how I want to love as you love! How I need your grace to be patient, to see the good side of others and not just the negative. Please teach me to do your will, to be your true disciple….* This asking can also take the form of confusion and complaint, as happens so often in the Book of Psalms: *Why, my God, have you forsaken me? Why do you let these things happen? Lord, I don't understand, teach me, enlighten me. Help me to go where you want me to go, because right now I don't feel like going there….*

As your consideration gives rise to these responses, the response will naturally come to a close and give way to a new consideration, and you will find yourself turning back to the meditation material. You may look again at the same highlight you just considered, or you may move on to something else, until a new consideration sparks a new response and a new topic of conversation. This exchange – this ongoing conversation in which you reflect on God's revelation and respond in your heart, with your own words – is the essence of Christian meditation. This is usually where the soul comes into its most intimate contact with Christ through the action of the Holy Spirit. Consideration is never enough; it must stir the heart to *Converse* with God.

During your meditation, then, you may often find yourself going back and forth between Steps 2 and 3, *Consider* and *Converse*. Just because you have considered one point and conversed with Christ about it doesn't mean you can't go back and consider it again from another angle, or consider another point, and then converse about that. The conversation is two-way;

you move back and forth between considering (listening) and responding, as much or as little as the Holy Spirit leads you.

Sometimes your response will be a torrent of words – so many that they tumble over each other as you struggle to express all that's in your heart. Other times you may find yourself simply repeating a short phrase, or even one word, and it says everything: *Lord... Jesus...* Sometimes, like the famous peasant of Ars, you will simply find yourself held by God's gaze and gazing back, and words, even in the silence of your heart, will be unnecessary. Whatever its specific form, this third step of your meditation, *Converse*, consists in letting down the guard around your heart, so that God's word for you today penetrates, regenerates, and inflames the most secret depths of who you are.

In this step of the meditation, you may also feel moved to converse with the saints and angels or the Blessed Virgin Mary, speaking with them about Christ, whom they know much better than you do, contemplating their example of fidelity to Christ, and asking for their intercession.

STEP 4: COMMIT

Towards the end of your meditation, it will be time for you to draw this heart-to-heart conversation to a close. There is a need to bring all the sentiments together, to wrap things up. Before you step back into life's hectic activity, you need to renew your commitment to the mission God has given you. In your prayer, he has renewed his call and now you renew your answer, accepting once again the life-project that gives meaning to your existence – that of following him, of imitating Christ by your fidelity to God's will in the big things as well as the small.

Usually this desire to renew your adherence to God's will flows naturally and easily out of the consideration and conversation stages. The renewal and deepening of your commitment to Christ and his kingdom, whether or not it is accompanied by intense feelings, is actually a prayer of adoration, worship, and love: *You know how weak I am, my Lord, but you also know how much I want to follow you. You have planted that desire in my heart: I am yours, Lord. Wherever I go, whatever happens, I belong to you. I never want to be separated from you. As hard as it is, I want to do your will, because you are God, my Creator and Redeemer, my Father and my faithful Friend. Thy will be done in my life today, Lord; thy kingdom come.*

You may even find yourself responding to your considerations with acts of adoration similar to those during the *Converse* stage of the meditation – this is fine. It doesn't mean you have to end your meditation right then. If you have time, you can go back and continue the consideration, or converse with other responses, like praise and gratitude. Then, at the end of the time you have set aside to meditate, you can return to this adoration, to this *Commit* step.[8]

If you can link this recommitment to the concrete tasks of

---

[8]*In both the Converse and the Commit steps, then, you find the traditional types, the traditional goals of prayer: Praise, Adoration, Sorrow, Thanksgiving, and Asking – P.A.S.T.A.*

your day, all the better. Most often, the daily meditation has followed themes connected to your program of spiritual work. In that case, you can recommit to following your program, or one particular point of your program, as a specific way of expressing your love for Christ. Sometimes, however, the Holy Spirit will nudge you towards a specific act of charity (i.e., visit your colleague who's in the hospital), or of self-governance (i.e., call your brother and apologize) – this too can give substance to your recommitment.

The meditation itself has glorified God and nourished your soul, regardless of any specific resolution you make in Step 4. The lifeblood of the meditation is your heart-to-heart conversation with the Lord, a conversation that puts you in contact with God and his grace, gradually transforming you into a mature Christian. You have deepened your friendship with Christ through spending this time with him. A new specific resolution may be an appropriate way to express this friendship at the end of the conversation, but often its most sincere expression is simply a renewal of your commitment to Christ and his kingdom, to the points of spiritual and apostolic work already on your agenda, and to the everyday tasks that are his will for you.

This fourth step is the bridge between prayer and action. If you are working on being more courageous about sharing your faith with your coworkers, you may finish your meditation by a commitment to put forth in a natural way the Christian point of view in today's conversations around the watercooler. If God has been leading you towards being a better spouse, you may renew your commitment to Christ by promising to avoid today that particular thing that you know really bothers your wife or husband. If you have been neglecting your prayer life, you may commit to giving your best attention to your daily Rosary in the evening. The specific form your recommitment takes will depend on the overall direction of your spiritual life. It doesn't have to be anything new (although it may be); it just has to be true.

Finish up your meditation by renewing your commitment to Christ in your own words. Then take a few moments to write down the lights God sent you during the meditation and thank him for them. Briefly go over how the meditation went. Did you follow the steps? Did anything in particular help you? Was there anything that hindered you? This brief analysis will help you get to know better each day what kind of pray-er you are, so that you can apply this knowledge in subsequent meditations, gradually learning to pray as God created you to pray.

It often helps to conclude your meditation with a short vocal prayer like the Our Father, the Hail Mary, the Anima Christi, or another favorite prayer of your own. There are some possibilities at the end of this guide.

Concentrate, Consider, Converse, and *Commit.* These are the four elements of a Christian meditation. The many books and manuals of prayer that enrich our Christian heritage offer numerous aids to meditation, and you should familiarize yourself with them and take advantage of them, but in the end, the methods and aids all tie into these four steps of prayer. This tried and true structure will give God more room to work in your soul than he would have if you only dedicated yourself to vocal prayer and spiritual reading.

DIFFICULTIES IN PRAYER

You will always face difficulties in prayer. Just accept it. The saints all experienced it, the Catechism teaches it, and theology confirms it. The difficulties stem from two sources – two unique qualities of your friendship with Christ.

1. First, this friendship is mediated by faith. You can't just call Jesus on the phone, as you can with your other friends. He is always with you, but your awareness of and access to his presence passes through faith. Faith is a virtue, which means that it can be more or less developed. The less developed it is, the more effort it takes to activate your awareness of God's presence. Many modern Christians have an underdeveloped faith. They have been unwittingly contaminated by the consumer culture's veneration for quantifiable evidence ("I won't believe it unless a scientific study proves it") and its elevation of feelings over reason ("I don't feel in love anymore, so why should I stay married?") – both of which weaken faith.

A scrawny faith often makes Jesus look fuzzy and seem distant, just as the sun seems weak and irrelevant when you're wearing dark glasses. Your ability to pray will suffer the consequences. Have you ever noticed how hard it is to be distracted when you watch a good movie? Effortlessly you pay perfect attention to a complex story for two hours. Contrast that with what typically happens during your fifteen minutes of meditation. What's the difference? Contact with God takes faith, "going as we do by faith and not by sight" (2 Cor 5:7). It takes the effort of "all your heart, soul, mind, and strength" (Mk 12:30) to align your fallen nature (which tends to seek fulfillment in the things of this earth) with the sublime truths that God has revealed through the teachings of the Church.

2. Your friendship with Christ is unique, not only by its mediation through faith, but also because the two friends are not equals. Christ is not just your friend; he is also your Creator, your Redeemer, and your Lord; he is all-wise and all-loving and he's trying to lead you along the steep and narrow path of Christian maturity. So, on your part, your relationship with him requires docility. But docility demands self-denial, which rubs your concupiscence the wrong way. Remember, baptism gave you back God's grace, but it didn't take away your deep-seated tendencies to selfishness (arrogance, independence, vanity, laziness, anger, lust, greed, etc.) that you inherited from original sin. Because of them, docility chafes. Sometimes the Good Shepherd leads you where you would rather not go, or pushes you farther along when you

would prefer to sit back and relax, or doesn't let you drink from a stream that looks fine to you. This divergence of wills makes prayer a constant battle.

SLOTH AND DISTRACTIONS The difficulties flowing from this need for faith and docility come in two basic varieties: *sloth* and *distractions*.

Sloth is spiritual laziness, distaste, and sluggishness in cultivating your relationship with God: *I can't pray before I go to work, because I need that extra few minutes of sleep; I can't go on a retreat since the playoffs start this weekend and I really want to watch them; I know I committed to begin praying the Rosary again, but I just don't feel like it, I have so much else to do....* Anything but spend time attending to the most important thing: your "vital and personal relationship with the living and true God,"[9] i.e., your life of prayer. That's sloth.

In the meditation itself, sloth can tempt you in numerous ways: procrastinating *(I'll do it later; I'll start meditating tomorrow)*, not getting your material ready ahead of time, giving in to tiredness, rushing through your preparatory acts instead of really concentrating, simply reading for most of the time instead of really engaging in the quest to consider and converse, or finishing with a vague and half-hearted commitment that really has no practical effect at all in your daily life or the pursuit of spiritual maturity. In these and many other ways, sloth slyly undermines the life of prayer.

---

[9]*Catechism of the Catholic Church*, 2558

Sloth *drains* energy from your spiritual life; distractions, on the other hand, *steer* that energy away from God. You go to Mass and sincerely want to worship God, but can't take your eyes off that family in the front pew that's making such a ruckus (or maybe you're part of that family); you pray the Rosary every day, but halfway through you realize that you have no idea which decade you're on because you're thinking about the budget presentation you have to make on Tuesday; you desperately try to spend some time every day in personal prayer, in Christian meditation, but you end up thinking about everything *except* God – family worries, upcoming engagements, temptations, pending bills and phone calls, job interviews, billboards, news stories…. They all violently and unremittingly claw at your attention as soon as you try to quiet your soul and attend to the Lord (more often than not, the devil has a hand in this). And sometimes when you pray, you're just plain bored. Welcome to the world of distractions.

SOLVING THE DIFFICULTIES The best defense against sloth and distractions is a good offense. Following a sound and simple meditation method like the one outlined above both flushes these temptations out of hiding – since you know clearly what you *should* be doing during your meditation, you catch yourself more easily as soon as you stop doing that – and also gives you a rudder and a lighthouse to navigate through their ambushes. But the method won't resolve the difficulties all by itself. You still have to steer the rudder and look to the lighthouse.

Temptations to sloth or distractions don't damage your prayer life – only *giving in* to temptations does that. In fact, each temptation is permitted by God because it gives you a chance for spiritual growth.

Take for example a temptation to slothfulness. The alarm clock goes off. Bleary-eyed, I wake up and the last thing I feel like doing is getting up to pray. If I cut out my fifteen-minute meditation, I can have fifteen minutes more sleep. How sweet that sounds! But wait a minute, why did I set my alarm to get up fifteen minutes earlier than I actually need to? Because I made a commitment; I resolved to start out my day with God because he is the purpose of my life and de-serves my praise and because I need his grace. A crisis of the heart has arisen: my feelings and habits of self-indulgence (egged on by the devil) tell me to hit the snooze button, roll over, and doze off again; my faith (animated by my guardian angel) tells me to turn off the alarm, throw back those cozy cov-ers, touch my bare feet down on that cold tile floor, and keep my appointment with God.

If God wanted to, he could resolve the crisis for me: he could push me out of bed, or make the bed disappear, or give me good feelings about prayer and bad feelings about staying in bed. But he doesn't, at least not usually. Rather, he leaves it up to me, nudging my conscience perhaps, but not forcing me either way. Here is where I can exercise the virtues of faith and docility, and in exercising them, strengthen them.

Distractions work the same way. I'm in the Blessed Sacrament chapel doing my daily meditation. Someone else comes through the door and enters the silent, sacred space. He takes a seat not too far away. I can't help noticing that he's wearing brand new tennis shoes. Are they Nikes or Reeboks? That reminds me about the marketing presentation I have to give this afternoon. My boss will be there. It's a critical account for the company…. Suddenly I realize that my mind is wandering.

Up to this point, I haven't been responsible for the distraction, because I wasn't even aware of it, but now I have three options: 1) I keep thinking about the presentation. After all, a lot is hanging on it, and my meditation is a bit dry anyway; 2) I get distracted by my distraction: "There I go again. Why can't I stay focused? I always get distracted. I am such an idiotic Christian, such a hypocrite. I'm so frustrated with myself…." 3) I calmly steer my attention back to my meditation, renewing my conviction that God and his action here matter far more than fruitless worrying about my presentation (which I have already prepared anyway), and that my tendency to get distracted affords me a new opportunity to exercise my faith and docility and turn back once again to my Lord.

Will I choose 1, 2, or 3? If I choose 3, then that distraction, which the devil wants to use to distance me from God, will actually have become an instrument of God's grace, drawing me closer to him and giving him glory. God allows temptations against my communion with God in order to afford me opportunities to deepen that communion.

The more closely you try to follow the 4-step method of meditation outlined above, the more you will get to know how these ubiquitous temptations try to derail your personal prayer life in particular, and the better equipped you will be to stay on track, using them to build up the virtues of faith and docility and become the pray-er God wants you to be.

HOW DO I KNOW IF I'M PRAYING WELL? We all tend to measure our prayer by our feelings: I prayed well if I *felt* God's presence, if I *felt* an emotional thrill. That's not the way to evaluate your prayer. Your relationship with Christ is a deep friendship built on faith and love. It goes much deeper than feelings. Feelings and emotions change with the weather, with our biorhythms, with our circumstances – they are often unpredictable and always undependable. Any friendship built on feelings, therefore, is doomed to frustration and failure. Mature Christians don't seek feelings or emotional states in their prayer. If God provides good feelings too, great, but the sincere Christian is after Christ: praising him, knowing him better, discovering what he wants, and renewing and deepening the decision to imitate him and follow him in the nitty-gritty of daily life, no matter the cost. Feelings are frills, but Christ is the core.

The fruit of a healthy prayer life takes time to grow and mature. Ultimately, it shows itself by growth in virtue, as you become more like Christ. Gradually, you grow in self-governance (controlling and channeling your instincts, passions, and basic human desires), prudence (seeing clearly what ought to be done in any particular situation and doing it), love (seeing others as Christ sees them and being able to sacrifice your own preferences for their sake), fortitude (taking on challenging tasks or projects for the sake of Christ's Kingdom and persevering through difficulties, obstacles, and opposition), and wisdom (detecting and relishing God's presence in all things and circumstances). Growth in these virtues takes place gradually, almost imperceptibly, on a day-to-day basis, just as a child slowly but surely grows into adulthood, or as plants mature in a garden. Meditation supplies much of the spiritual nutrients that cause these virtues to grow.

On any given day, then, measuring whether your meditation went well or badly is not so easy. Your meditation may have been quite pleasing to God and full of grace for your soul even when it was unpleasant and difficult from a strictly emotional perspective. An athlete may have a great practice session even though it was painful and frustrating – likewise with a daily meditation.

You'll find some helpful indicators below. The most important thing, though, is simply to keep striving to pray better. Speak about your prayer life in spiritual direction and confession, and trust that if you are sincerely doing your best, the Holy Spirit will do the rest.

MY MEDITATION WENT BADLY WHEN I...

- Didn't plan ahead regarding what material I would use, when and where I would meditate, making sure to turn off my cell phone, etc.

- Simply gave in to the many distractions that vied for my attention

- Let myself fall asleep

- Skipped over the first step, *Concentrate*, or did it sloppily; how can my prayer go well if I am not keenly aware of God's presence?

- Didn't humbly ask God to help me and to give me whatever graces I need to continue growing in my spiritual life

- Spent the whole time reading, thinking, or daydreaming and didn't stop to ask what God was saying *to me* and then respond from my heart

- Tried to stir up warm, fuzzy feelings and intense emotions instead of conversing heart-to-heart on the level of faith

- Didn't renew my commitment to Christ and his Kingdom at the end of the meditation

- Shortened the time I had committed to without a really important reason

MY MEDITATION WENT WELL WHEN I...

- Actually fulfilled the commitment I made to spend a certain amount of time in meditation every day

- Faithfully followed the methodology in spite of tiredness, distractions, dryness, or any other difficulty (or if it was impossible to follow the four-step method, did my best to give praise to God in whatever way I could throughout my meditation time)

- Stayed with the points of consideration that struck me most as long as I found material there for reflection and conversation

- Sought only to know and love Christ better, so as to be able to follow him better

- Made sure to speak to Christ from my heart about whatever I was meditating on (or whatever was most on my heart), even when it was hard to find the words

- Was completely honest in my conversation – I didn't say things to God just out of routine or because I wanted to impress him with my eloquence; I told him what was really in my heart

- Made a sincere effort to listen to what God was saying to me throughout the time of prayer, seeking applications for my own life, circumstances, needs, and challenges

- Finished the meditation more firmly convinced of God's goodness and more firmly committed to doing my best to follow him faithfully

A SAMPLE MEDITATION

The paragraphs below are adapted from a meditation directed by Father Anthony Bannon, LC, and taken with permission from www.vocation.com. Although everyone prays a little bit differently from everyone else, reading through a real meditation from start to finish can help these ideas come into focus. Comments are included in italics.

STEP 1: CONCENTRATE *I come into the place where I will be meditating. I remind myself that God is truly present, here and everywhere, that he is watching over me and listening to me, eager to spend this time together; he sees into the depths of my heart. Then I kneel or sit, make the sign of the cross, and address him.*

I thank you, Father, for the immense love you showed me in creating me and redeeming me, giving me this time with you, spending this time with me, intervening in my life. I know you have something to say to me today. I want hear it; I need to hear it. I want to love you in a real way, not abstractly or in theory only. I want to love you today, and not tomorrow. I want to love you here where you have placed me and not somewhere else in my dreams. I want to love you in your Church. I want to love you in the people that you place in my path.

STEP 2: CONSIDER *First, I read the Gospel passage, then I read it again, more slowly, picturing it, paying attention to whichever words jump out at me. Maybe something strikes me right away, and I stay with that, considering it and letting it lead me into a conversation with Christ.*

Gospel Passage: Matthew 13:47-50

"The Kingdom of Heaven is like a dragnet that is cast into the sea and brings in a haul of all kinds of fish. When it is full, the fishermen haul it ashore. And then sitting down they collect the good ones in baskets and throw away those that are no use. This is how it will be at the end of time. The angels will appear and separate the wicked from the upright, to throw them into the blazing furnace where there will be weeping and grinding of teeth."

Maybe one thing that strikes you after reading the passage is a consideration like the following:

Unlike the previous parables in this chapter, which described the kingdom as already present, this one describes the kingdom as something still to come. Jesus speaks about the relationship between this kingdom of God and the future life at the end of time. And Jesus seems to want to get across to us one particular message. "The kingdom is like a dragnet that is cast into the sea and brings in a haul of all kinds of fish." The end of time is just as unexpected for us as a net that drops into the water and is pulled along behind the boat is for the fish it catches. Just as sudden as that…

STEP 3: CONVERSE *After making that reflection, you may naturally find yourself wanting to converse with Christ about it, simply and sincerely, as follows, for example:*

I know and I believe that the end of the world will come, that you will judge me and everyone. And yet, I really don't think about it very much. You thought about it a lot. You often spoke about it. Lord, you know all things; you are

Wisdom itself. I thank you for this reminder that the end will come. You want me to be ready. You want me to keep the end in mind. I want to too. I don't want to live like an animal, interested only in satisfying my momentary desires. No, I want to live in the light of your truth. I believe in the power of your truth. Lord Jesus, enlighten me, guide me, never stop teaching me how you want me to live.

STEP 2 AGAIN: CONSIDER *After I have had my say and spoken what is in my heart, I turn my attention back to the Lord's word to see what else he has to say to me. I have already sought material for reflection and conversation in the passage itself, and I don't seem to find any more. So now I move on to the commentary. I read one section of the commentary, which points out something I may have overlooked. It sparks another personal reflection, so I pause and consider it – what it means, what it tells me about Christ, what it means for me, how it applies to my hopes and struggles:*

Prewritten Commentary

When it is full, the fishermen haul the net ashore. Then they do the all-important thing: they sit down and start sorting out their catch. They keep the good fish and throw away the useless ones. And Jesus said, "This is the way it is going to be at the end of time. The Angels will appear and separate the wicked from the upright." At the end of time, the angels won't simply check and see how God has made us, and separate us according to the qualities that God has given us. Instead, their criteria will be our own wickedness and uprightness. In other words, we will be judged according to what we have done with those things that God has given us, whether we have used them wickedly (selfishly) or uprightly.

A personal reflection sparked by that commentary could be something like this:

PERSONAL CONSIDERATION OF THE COMMENTARY

What do the angels recognize in each one of those people? They recognize which ones are members of Christ's kingdom; they see signs of that in each person's heart, each person's character, which was formed by the choices they made throughout their lifetime.

I will be one of those fish, one of those people. Will the angels recognize in me the signs of the kingdom that Jesus has talked about in the previous parables? Will they see in me someone who searched for the fine pearl, recognized its value and beauty, and had the good sense to sell everything else in order to possess it? Will they see me as someone who recognized the treasure in the field and sold everything else in order to buy it? When the angels find me, will they recognize in me the leaven that uplifted the people around me? Will they see in me someone who spent his whole life transforming the world around him, transforming himself as he served those around him, or will they find me no different from those I should have changed? Will they find just the flat dough of the world in my life, unrisen?

STEP 3 AGAIN: CONVERSE *At some point while you consider whatever struck you in the commentary, you may find yourself wanting to respond directly to the Lord, to say something in* *response to what the Holy Spirit has been saying to you through your consideration. If nothing comes spontaneously, as your time for meditation draws to its close, you will need to purposely transition into a conversation. Remember, consideration only matters insofar as it draws you into a heart-to-heart conversation with God. Your response to God that emerges out of the above consideration may look something like this:*

Lord Jesus, I thank you for speaking this parable, because so often I get too caught up with the urgent cares of today and the apparent difficulty of following you. I forget that all of this will come to an end and that you have a bigger plan in mind.

You invite me to look at what is coming in the future life, to be ready for the dragnet. You ask me to look at heaven, which is awaiting me. Lord, I can only live as your faithful disciple, as a member of your kingdom, with the help of your grace. I can only persevere with your help. Please never let me lose sight of the hopes and expectations that you have for me – you really do have a dream for my life; this parable reminds me that you do. The greatest thing that I can do, the greatest thing I will ever see will be the joy on your face if you can one day say to me, "Well done, good and faithful servant." Then you will be able to receive me as you want to receive me, among the upright, and bring me into the true kingdom of heaven.

STEP 4: COMMIT *As your meditation time comes to an end, you need to recommit yourself to Christ in light of what the Holy*

Spirit has been showing you through your considerations and conversation. Most importantly, you want to refocus your most basic attitudes: you are a follower of Christ and God's will is the path of your life. You can also translate that focused attitude into a concrete commitment; e.g., in accordance with your program of spiritual work or in accordance with a particular circumstance you will be facing today. You also wrap up the meditation itself, thanking God for the graces you have received, and asking forgiveness for your distractions and shortcomings. For this meditation, your recommitment may look something like this:

Jesus, you know that I want to live as a true Christian, with my sights set on your kingdom. Whatever you ask me today, I will do, if you give me the strength I need to do it. I know I will need your strength to be patient with my coworkers, and to give myself eagerly to this tedious project at work. If I stay faithful to your will, to my conscience and to these normal duties of my state in life, and if I live your will with love and gratitude in my heart, then I will be ready for the last day, whenever you decide to bring it along. And don't let me hide my faith in my conversation at lunch today. Jesus, they need to know you as much as I do; make me a good messenger. Thy will be done, Lord, not mine.

Thank you, Lord, for being with me in this meditation. Thank you for the good thoughts, the good affections, and the beginnings of good resolutions that you have placed in my heart. I am sorry for the moments I have been distracted, gone off on tangents, been less attentive to your presence. Grant me in some other way any graces that I might have missed. And I also pray for each one of my brothers and sisters: I pray for each one who wants to follow you. Our Father…

SOME POSSIBLE PREPARATORY AND CONCLUDING PRAYERS

PREPARATORY PRAYERS These are provided as examples and helps. Sometimes you may need help during Step 1 of your meditation, *Concentrate*. These small prayers express the attitudes that you need to stir up at the start of your meditation. They can also sometimes serve as material for *Consider* and *Converse* as well.

1. ENTERING INTO GOD'S PRESENCE

My Lord and my God, I firmly believe that you are present here and everywhere, that you are looking upon me and listening to me, and that you see into the very depths of my soul. You are my Creator, my Redeemer, and my Father. I believe in your love for me. You never take your eyes off me. You have something to say to me today. Your love for me never grows weary. You never stop drawing close to me and drawing me closer to you.

Lord, who am I to place myself in your presence? I am a poor creature unworthy of appearing before you, and yet amid all my misery I adore you devoutly. I ask you to forgive my many sins.

Jesus, teach me to pray. Direct my prayer, so that it may rise to your throne like fragrant incense. Let all the thoughts of my spirit and my heart's inmost sentiments be directed towards serving and praising God in a perfect way. I need to hear your Word for me today, and I long to hear it. You know how much I need you, how much I want to follow you. Grant me in this prayer the grace of knowing you better, loving you more, and becoming more like you. Grant me the grace I most need.

My loving Mother Mary, my holy guardian angel, angels and saints in heaven: intercede for me so that this prayer will help me and all the other people connected to my life.

2. TRADITIONAL ACTS OF FAITH, HOPE, AND LOVE

Act of Faith

My God, I firmly believe all that you have revealed and that the Holy Church puts before us to be believed, for you are the infallible truth, who does not deceive and cannot be deceived. I expressly believe in you, the only true God in three equal and distinct persons, the Father, Son, and Holy Spirit. And I believe in Jesus Christ, Son of God, who took flesh and died for us, and who will give to each one, according to his merits, eternal reward or punishment. I always want to live in accordance with this faith. Lord, increase my faith.

Act of Hope

My God, by virtue of your promises and the merits of Jesus Christ, our Savior, I hope to receive from your goodness eternal life and the necessary grace to merit it with the good deeds I am required and propose to do. Lord, may I be able to delight in you forever.

Act of Love

My God, I love you with all my heart and above all things, because you are infinitely good and our eternal happiness; for your sake, I love my neighbor as I love myself and I forgive the offenses I have received. Lord, grant that I will love you more and more.

Petition

My God, here present now, hear and guide my prayer, and lead me to the verdant pastures and refreshing waters of your Truth and your Love.

3. ENTERING INTO GOD'S PRESENCE THROUGH ACTS OF GRATITUDE AND HUMILITY

My Lord and my God, you are infinitely kind and merciful. I thank you with all my heart for the countless gifts you have given me, especially for creating and redeeming me, for calling me to the Catholic faith and to my vocation, and for freeing me from so many dangers of soul and body.

You have shown me the door that leads to heaven, to being one with you forever. What am I? Mere sand. And so, why have you sought me out, why have you loved me, why have you shown me that door? Why did you become flesh and leave me your Gospel? Because you love me. I want to thank you for everything you did for me, and all that you do for me. In this prayer I want to praise and glorify you.

How I need your grace! Please guide me now. Teach me to know, love, and do your will for me. I am nothing without you; I am no one without you, but I know that with you all things are possible.

4. IN THE CONTEXT OF SEEKING GOD'S WILL

My Lord and my God, you are Love itself, and the source of all love and goodness. Out of love you created me to know you, love you, and serve you in a unique way, as no one else can. I believe that you have a plan for my life, that you have a task in your kingdom reserved just for me. Your plan and your task are far better than any other I might choose: they will glorify you, fulfill the desires of my heart, and save those souls who are depending on my generous response.

Lord, grant me the light I need to see the next step in that plan; grant me the generosity I need to set aside my own plans in favor of yours; and grant me the strength I need to put my hands to your plough and never turn back. You know me better than I know myself, so you know that I am sinful and weak. All the more reason that I need your grace to uphold the good desires you have planted in my heart, O Lord!

Make my prayer today pleasing to you. Show me your will for me, O gentle and eternal God, and help me to say with Mary, "I am the servant of the Lord; let it be done to me according to your word," and to say with Jesus, "Let not my will be done, but yours."

5. RECALLING CHRIST'S PERSONAL LOVE FOR ME

Lord, you wished to create me. I would not exist were it not for your almighty power. You created me because you love me, and I want to love you the way you have loved me. Lord, two thousand years ago mankind walked the earth in darkness, lost by the sin of our first parents. And you, in obedience to the Father and out of love for me, decided to become flesh in the Virgin's womb. You became a man so as to suffer for me, redeem me from my sins, and open the gates of heaven for me. Thank you for your love, Jesus; thank you for being born of the Blessed Virgin. Thank you, dear Mother, for saying yes to God and allowing the Second Person of the Blessed Trinity, Jesus Christ, to become man.

Lord Jesus, you are here with me now. You came into the world to teach me. You left me the path I must take to reach you and possess you forever in the Gospel. Thank you, Jesus, for such love. You truly are almighty God. I am a poor and miserable creature; and yet you loved me and continue to love me, not only in words, but with real love: love shown in works. That is why I know that you are with me now, in my heart, watching over me. Guide my prayer, Lord, cleanse my soul of all my sins and selfishness and fill it with your light and your love. Grant me the grace I need most, because without you, I can do nothing.

6. FROM THE CHURCH'S RICH LITURGICAL TRADITION

THE TE DEUM

You are God: we praise; you are the Lord: we acclaim you; you are the eternal Father: all creation worships you. To you all angels, all the powers of heaven, Cherubim and Seraphim, sing in endless praise: Holy, holy, holy, Lord, God of power and might, heaven and earth are full of your glory. The glorious company of apostles praises you, the noble fellowship of prophets praises you, the white-robed army of martyrs praises you. Throughout the world, the holy Church acclaims you: Father, of majesty unbounded, your true and only Son, worthy of all worship, and the Holy Spirit, advocate and guide.

You, Christ, are the King of glory, the eternal Son of the Father. When you became man to set us free, you did not spurn the Virgin's womb. You overcame the sting of death and opened the kingdom of heaven to all believers. You are seated at God's right hand in glory. We believe that you will come and be our judge.

Come then, Lord, and help your people, bought with the price of your own blood, and bring us with your saints to glory everlasting. Save your people, Lord, and bless your inheritance. Govern and uphold them now and always. Day by day, we bless you. We praise your name forever. Keep us today, Lord, from all sin. Have mercy on us, Lord, have mercy. Lord, show us your love and mercy, for we put our trust in you. In you, Lord is our hope: and we shall never hope in vain. Lord, hear my prayer, and let my cry reach you.

PREFACES TO THE EUCHARISTIC PRAYER, SUNDAYS IN ORDINARY TIME I

Father, all-powerful and ever-living God, we do well always and everywhere to give you thanks through Jesus Christ our Lord. Through his cross and resurrection, he freed us from sin and death and called us to the glory that has made us a chosen race, a royal priesthood, a holy nation, a people set apart. Everywhere we proclaim your mighty works, for you have called us out of darkness into your own wonderful light.

PREFACE TO THE FOURTH EUCHARIST PRAYER

Father in heaven, it is right that we should give you thanks and glory: you are the one God, living and true. Through all eternity, you live in unapproachable light. Source of life and goodness, you have created all things, to fill your creatures with every blessing and lead all men to the joyful vision of your light. Countless hosts of angels stand before you to do your will; they look upon your splendor and praise you night and day.

CONCLUDING PRAYERS Once you have renewed your commitment to follow Christ and expressed that in your own words and in a concrete resolution, briefly reviewed how your meditation went, and jotted down the insights God gave you (Step 4, *Commit*), it often helps to wrap up your meditation with a short, ready-made prayer that sums things up. St. Ignatius of Loyola used to finish with the Our Father, the Hail Mary, and the Glory Be. Here are some other options, in case you still haven't found your personal favorites. It is customary to end the meditation with the Sign of the Cross.

PRAYER OF DEDICATION

Lord Jesus,
I give you my hands to do your work.
I give you my feet to follow your way.
I give you my eyes to see as you do.
I give you my tongue to speak your words.
I give you my mind so you can think in me.
I give you my spirit so you can pray in me.
Above all, I give you my heart
So in me you can love your Father and all people.
I give you my whole self so you can grow in me,
Till it is you, Lord Jesus,
Who lives and works and prays in me.
Amen.

PRAYER TO THE HOLY SPIRIT

Holy Spirit,
Inspire in me
What I should think,
What I should say,
What I should leave unsaid,
What I should write,
What I should do
And how I should act
To bring about the good of souls,
The fulfillment of my mission,
And the triumph of the Kingdom of Christ.
Amen.

LEAD KINDLY LIGHT

Lead, kindly Light, amid the encircling gloom,
Lead thou me on;
The night is dark, and I am far from home,
Lead thou me on.
Keep thou my feet; I do not ask to see
The distant scene; one step enough for me.

I was not ever thus, nor prayed that thou
Shouldst lead me on;
I loved to choose and see my path; but now
Lead thou me on.
I loved the garish day, and, spite of fears,
Pride ruled my will: remember not past years.

So long thy power hath blest me, sure it still
Will lead me on.
O'er moor and fen, o'er crag and torrent, till
The night is gone,
And with the morn those Angel faces smile,
Which I have loved long since, and lost awhile.

- Venerable J.H. Newman (1801-1890)

FROM ST. PATRICK'S BREASTPLATE

I bind unto myself today
The strong name of the Trinity:
By invocation of the same,
The Three in One and One in Three

Christ be with me, Christ within me,
Christ behind me, Christ before me,
Christ beside me, Christ to win me,
Christ to comfort and restore me.
Christ beneath me, Christ above me,
Christ in quiet, Christ in danger,
Christ in hearts of all that love me,
Christ in mouth of friend and stranger.

Praise to the Lord of my salvation –
Salvation is of Christ the Lord!

- Ascribed to St Patrick of Ireland (circa 450 A.D.)

PRAYER OF SELF-DEDICATION TO JESUS CHRIST

Take, Lord, and receive
all my liberty, my understanding, my whole will,
all I have and all I possess.
You gave it all to me; to you, Lord, I return it all.
It is all yours: Do with me entirely as you will.
Give me your love and your grace:
This is enough for me. Amen.

- St. Ignatius of Loyola (1491-1556)

PRAYER OF ST. FRANCIS

Lord, make me an instrument of Your peace.
Where there is hatred, let me sow love;
where there is injury, pardon;
where there is doubt, faith;
where there is despair, hope;
where there is darkness, light;
and where there is sadness, joy.

O, Divine Master,
grant that I may not so much seek
to be consoled as to console;
to be understood as to understand;
to be loved as to love;
for it is in giving that we receive;
it is in pardoning that we are pardoned;
and it is in dying that we are born to eternal life. Amen.

- St Francis of Assisi (1181-1226)

LITANY OF HUMILITY

This prayer renews one's commitment to follow Christ's summary for Christian living: "Set your hearts on his kingdom first, and on his righteousness, and all these other things will be given you as well" (Mt 6:33). It should be prayed from that perspective.

Jesus, meek and humble of heart, hear me!
From the desire of being esteemed, *Lord Jesus, free me!*

From the desire of being loved…
From the desire of being acclaimed…
From the desire of being honored…
From the desire of being praised…
From the desire of being preferred…
From the desire of being consulted…
From the desire of being approved…
From the desire of being valued…

From the fear of being humbled, *Lord Jesus, free me!*
From the fear of being despised…
From the fear of being dismissed…
From the fear of being rejected…
From the fear of being defamed…
From the fear of being forgotten…
From the fear of being ridiculed…
From the fear of being wronged…
From the fear of being suspected…
From resenting that my opinion is not followed…

That others will be more loved than I, *Lord Jesus, make this my prayer!*
That others will be esteemed more than I…

That others will increase in the opinion of the world while I diminish…
That others will be chosen while I am set aside…
That others will be praised while I am overlooked…
That others will be preferred to me in everything…

Lord Jesus, though you were God, you humbled yourself to the extreme of dying on a cross, to set an enduring example to the shame of my arrogance and vanity. Help me to learn your example and put it into practice so that, by humbling myself in accordance with my lowliness here on earth, you can lift me up to rejoice in you forever in heaven. Amen.

- Cardinal Merry del Val, Secretary of State under Pope St Pius X (1865-1930)

MISSION PRAYER

Lord, you have created me to do you some definite service; you have committed some work to me which you have not committed to another. I have my mission—I never may know it in this life, but I shall be told it in the next. Somehow I am necessary for your purposes, as necessary in my place as an Archangel in his—if, indeed, I fail, you can raise another, as you could make the stones children of Abraham. Yet I have a part in this great work; I am a link in a chain, a bond of connection between persons. You have not created me for naught. I shall do good, I shall do your work; I shall be an angel of peace, a preacher of truth in my own place, while not intending it, if I do but your commandments and serve you in my calling.

Therefore I will trust you. Whatever, wherever I am, I can never be thrown away. If I am in sickness, my sickness may serve you; in perplexity, my perplexity may serve you; if I am in sorrow, my sorrow may serve you. My sickness, or perplexity, or sorrow may be necessary causes of some great end, which is quite beyond me. You do nothing in vain; you may prolong my life, you may shorten it; you know what you are about; you may take away my friends, you may throw me among strangers, you may make me feel desolate, make my spirits sink, hide the future from me—still you know what you are about.

- Adapted from a reflection composed by
Venerable J.H. Newman (1801-1890)

MORE FROM THE CHURCH'S RICH LITURGICAL TRADITION

THE GLORIA

Glory to God in the highest and peace to his people on earth.
Lord God, heavenly King, almighty God, and Father,
   we worship you, we give you thanks,
   we praise you for your glory.
Lord Jesus Christ, only Son of the Father,
Lord God, Lamb of God,
You take away the sin of the world:
   have mercy on us;
You are seated at the right hand of the Father:
   receive our prayer.
For you alone are the Holy One, you alone are the Lord,

You alone are the Most High, Jesus Christ,
  with the Holy Spirit,
In the Glory of God the Father.
Amen.

THE APOSTLES' CREED

I believe in God, the Father almighty, creator of heaven and earth. I believe in Jesus Christ, his only Son, our Lord. He was conceived by the power of the Holy Spirit and born of the Virgin Mary. He suffered under Pontius Pilate, was crucified, died, and was buried. He descended to the dead. On the third day he rose again. He ascended into heaven, and is seated at the right hand of the Father. He will come again to judge the living and the dead. I believe in the Holy Spirit, the holy catholic Church, the communion of saints, the forgiveness of sins, the resurrection of the body, and the life everlasting. Amen.